Berty Ashley is a molecular biologist with the Dystrophy Annihilation Research Trust. He works with rare genetic disorders. What is not rare, though, is to see him conducting quizzes or attending them. He is the author of the popular 'Easy Like Sunday Morning' series of quizzes published in *The Hindu*'s *Sunday Magazine*. He was the senior content editor for two seasons of the Tamil edition of 'Kaun Banega Crorepati'. He is also a lover of music—not only playing but collecting, as is evident by his growing stack of vinyl records of jazz, prog, Hindustani and heavy metal music. He and his partner, Akhila, live in Bengaluru, surrounded by books, music and an assortment of pens and guitars.

Akhila Phadnis is a freelance translator. She holds a master's in Translation Studies from Durham University, the UK, and in Psychology from Madras University, Chennai, Tamil Nadu. She enjoys reading, practising calligraphy, learning new languages, quizzing, playing board games and taking long walks by the beach.

The Amazing NATURE QUIZ

**BERTY ASHLEY
AND
AKHILA PHADNIS**

Published by
Rupa Publications India Pvt. Ltd 2019
7/16, Ansari Road, Daryaganj
New Delhi 110002

Sales centres:
Allahabad Bengaluru Chennai
Hyderabad Jaipur Kathmandu
Kolkata Mumbai

Copyright © Berty Ashley and Akhila Phadnis 2019

The views and opinions expressed in this book are the authors' own and the facts are as reported by him which have been verified to the extent possible, and the publishers are not in any way liable for the same.

All rights reserved.
No part of this publication may be reproduced, stored in a retrieval system, or transmitted, in any form or by any means, electronic, mechanical, photocopying, recording or otherwise, without the prior permission of the publishers.

ISBN: 978-93-5333-718-6

First impression 2019

10 9 8 7 6 5 4 3 2 1

The moral right of the authors has been asserted.

Printed at HT Media Ltd, Gr. Noida

This book is sold subject to the condition that it shall not, by way of trade or otherwise, be lent, resold, hired out, or otherwise circulated, without the publisher's prior consent, in any form of binding or cover other than that in which it is published.

CONTENTS

Introduction — *vii*

1. Brilliant Bacteria — 1
2. Blissful Birds — 9
3. Packed with Plants — 16
4. Fantastic Flowers and Terrific Trees — 23
5. Beasts in Books — 30
6. Memorable Mammals — 36
7. Rocking Reptiles and Astonishing Amphibians — 43
8. Interesting Insects — 50
9. Magnificent Marine Life — 57
10. Superlative Specimens — 64
11. Phrases and Idioms — 72
12. Wacky Wildlife — 77

Acknowledgements — 85

INTRODUCTION

Come forth into the light of things, let nature be your teacher.

—William Wordsworth

Nature is something that is unique to life on earth. It encompasses all living things that have lived, thrived and died through a billion years of existence on this planet. As of the time of writing, the authors (to the best of their knowledge) know of no other place in the universe that has nature. Unfortunately, this unique entity is taken for granted by one of those very animals that are a product of nature, humankind. We, as humans, have, over the years, exploited and exhausted earth's natural resources, and in the process, devastated its natural elements, which are dependent on those very resources. Man has single-handedly caused the extinction of more natural species than any other organism in earth's long history. We have lost animals and plants that a huge proportion of the population does not even know existed. The beauty of nature, though long-lasting, is incapable of enduring the constant onslaught by successive generations of humans. The only way we can bring about a change for the better is by raising awareness, especially among the younger generation. Both authors of this book have felt immensely connected with nature since they were children and owe it to the people who taught them and introduced them to this world. This is our way of carrying on that legacy, our humble way of passing on that love for all things natural in the form of thought-provoking and fact-filled questions.

We do not want you to finish off these sets at record speed; we do not want you to try and get every answer right; we would be happiest if you were to read a question and stop, ponder over the information, look it up online, see if you could find out more information about the same. If the subject is in a threatened condition, see if there is a way for you to contribute to its conservation. You could check with the local wildlife expert or resource. Volunteer to be part of a team that collects data on the subject. Do not undermine what one person can do; you might not realize it, but you can be that single person who accelerates conservation of the environment. Right now, governments all around the world are going both ways. They are either stepping-up their game to save nature by banning plastic, cleaning-up ecosystems and pumping much-needed funds into conservation projects or (scarily) denying climate change, opening up natural resources to greedy corporates, siphoning money away from conservation projects and destroying data that could help future generations.

The authors believe that with a substantial number of people who are aware and armed with facts, we will be able to tackle those who are destroying our planet. We have the earth; it has water, wind and fire. All it needs is the hearts of humans united in saving it. Ignorance is our worst enemy, but in this case, you cannot escape from nature. As the great J.R.R. Tolkien said, 'The wide world is all about you: you can fence yourselves in, but you cannot forever fence it out.'

We hope this book* inspires you to learn more about the wonders of nature and further inspires you to do something to ensure it stays that way for future generations to enjoy as well.

---

*Some of the questions in this book first appeared in *The Hindu*'s *Sunday Magazine* quiz called 'Easy Like Sunday Morning'.

1. BRILLIANT BACTERIA

1. *Magnetospirillum magneticum* is a corkscrew-shaped bacterium that collects iron from its environment and makes magnetite nanocrystals in little sacs. These crystals are then arranged in a straight line by the cellular skeleton. This leads to the bacteria being naturally aligned by the action of the earth. The bacterium then follows this line up and down, without getting lost, knowing exactly where it was. Thanks to this fantastic ability, these bacteria are referred to by the name of a device that humans use in the same way. What device, which humans only learned to use in 200 BC, have these bacteria been emulating for millions of years?

2. *Pseudomonas syringae* is a rod-shaped bacterium, which can infect a wide range of plants. It gets its name from the tree it was first isolated from, the Lilac (*Syringa vulgaris*). An interesting characteristic of this bacterium is its ability to produce Ice Nucleation Active (INA) proteins, which cause the water inside

plants to freeze, leading to injury. Recently, a study concluded that this bacterium plays a huge part in a certain weather phenomenon. Consequently, the INA proteins are used to make an artificial version of the same. What item, which is used in resorts in mountains, is made using the proteins obtained from this bacterium?

3. This bacterium was named for the German-Austrian paediatrician who isolated a variety of these bacteria from infant fecal samples by using his own anaerobic culture methods in the early 1900s. He initially named them *Bacterium coli commune*, but in 1919, it was named after him. It makes up around 0.1 per cent of the microbes found in our intestines and produces vitamin K2. Under certain circumstances, it could cause food poisoning in the hosts. Due to its phenomenal growth cycle, in which it can reproduce in twenty minutes, it is the most widely studied prokaryotic model organism. The fields of biotechnology and microbiology are indebted to it, as it has served as the host organism for the majority of work with the recombinant DNA. What is the name of this very important bacterium?

4. *Geobacter metallireducens* is a bacterium that oxidizes several short-chain fatty acids, alcohols and monoaromatic compounds and can use uranium for its growth. It has a unique ability to give away a subatomic particle to metal substances by a process

called reduction. Thanks to this amazing ability, *G. metallireducens* is being studied as a possible way to treat industrial sites, where 'cyanide-metal complexes' have formed to contaminate the site. What fundamental particle can this microbe lose?

5. *Aliivibrio* is a genus of bacteria that has a symbiotic relationship with a certain marine animal. A young specimen of this animal collects these bacteria in a special cavity in its underbelly. There, the bacteria are adept at swimming through the mucus and lives off the sugar and protein in the mucus. In return, the bacteria glow with a blue-green light. Thanks to this, the animal blends in with the moonlight and can cruise around undetected by predators. What animal is this, which, though it has blue-green bacteria, produces a black-coloured ink?

6. *Acidithiobacillus* are usually found in mines where they live in slimy 'snottites'. These bacteria live off sulphur, iron and pyrite. They are also responsible for the characteristic sparkle in caves. They digest these metals and excrete a liquid that dissolves limestone, creating tiny gypsum crystals. What does *Acidithiobacillus* excrete, which your chemistry teacher would have sternly asked you to stay away from in school?

7. Bacteria are single-celled organisms, but that doesn't mean they lack the ability to coordinate and work together. The *Myxococcus xanthus* bacteria travel in a

wandering, rippling swarm that scientists refer to as a '____ ____'. The swarm crawls around and on finding a victim, releases antibiotics to paralyze it and then releases digestive enzymes to break it down. This name refers to an animal that travels in packs and was one of the first animals to be domesticated by humans. What is the name for this swarm of bacteria, a term made famous by the movie *The Hangover*?

8. 'X' Agar is an enriched growth medium used for isolation of pathogenic bacteria. It is a version of the blood agar plate, but in this case, the red blood cells have been lysed slowly by heating them to 80 °C. The name of the agar comes from its almost brown colour, which is obtained after lysing the blood cells and not because of the presence of any popular edible product. What is the name of this microbiological entity, which, though sounds yummy, under no circumstances should be ingested?

9. *Photorhabdus luminescens* is a pathogenic bacterium that is lethal to insects. Inside an insect, it produces toxins that kill it, enzymes that liquefy it, and antibiotics that prevent any other microbes from getting in on the feast. During this entire process, it glows with a bright green colour. During the American Civil War, it used to get into the wounds of soldiers but because of the antibiotics it produced, it kept the wounds clean and didn't allow other microbes to infect them. This led to

the soldiers calling it by a certain name because they believed that God had sent his messengers to tend to their wounds. By what name was *P. luminescens* known to Civil War soldiers?

10. *Yersinia pestis* is a rod-shaped bacterium that was first isolated by Alexandre Yersin in 1894. He gave it the name 'pestis' as a reference to the Latin 'pestilentia', from which we get another word in English that refers to a particular epidemic. *Y. pestis* causes that particular epidemic and has been reported to have been the cause of the highest number of human deaths in history. During the fourteenth century AD, the bacterium was responsible for the death of at least one-third of the population of Europe. Thanks to modern medicine, the epidemic is under control. Which disease does the bacteria cause and what word shares its origin with it?

11. *Wolbachia* is genus of bacteria that is possibly the most common reproductive parasite in the world. It infects the most populous group of animals on the planet. Studies have shown that almost 70 per cent of these animals are potential hosts for the bacteria. *Wolbachia* have multiple effects on these animals, including rendering the host asexual, killing off an entire gender, inserting its entire genome into the cell, and in some cases, even having a symbiotic relationship where the animal cannot function properly without the infection.

What group of animals that vastly outnumber humans is affected by the *Wolbachia* species?

12. Superbugs are resistant to all antibiotics and are a huge threat to medicine. One mechanism, which contributes to antibiotic resistance, involves an enzyme called NDM-1. This is responsible for resistance to *Klebsiella pneumoniae*. NDM-1 was first observed in a Swedish man who fell sick after visiting a country. Though it was later seen in other places, the name stuck. M stands for 'Metallo-beta-lactamase-1'. ND stands for a place, which is also referenced in a 2011-cult Bollywood film starring Imran Khan. What does ND stand for and what was the movie?

13. *Deinococcus radiodurans* is a polyextremophilic bacterium, which can survive cold, dehydration, vacuum and acid. According to *The Guinness Book of World Records*, it is listed as the world's toughest bacterium. It gets its name from its extraordinary ability to withstand extremely high doses (up to 2,500 times higher) of a certain nature that is fatal to human beings even in small doses. This amazing ability is thanks to an incredible DNA repair mechanism it possesses. What can this microscopic bacterium survive that makes it so special?

14. *Candidatus Desulforudis audaxviator* is a unique bacterium that is found 3 kilometres below the Earth's surface, where it has survived for millions of years on

energy sourced from the radioactive decay of minerals in the surrounding rocks. The bacterium is one of the few known organisms that grow without depending on sunlight. The bacterium gives scientists an idea of how life would have been billions of years ago when the first bacteria had formed. While mining for which precious commodity in South Africa was this even more precious bacteria found?

15. This bacterium is the only obligate pathogen in the genus Bacillus and is a gram-positive endospore-forming bacterium. It causes an infection that generates black blisters and is spread by contact with the bacterium's spores. Although the bacteria has killed thousands of people and animals, it has only recently kindled major interest after some countries developed it as a bioweapon. The bacterium also lends its name to the only band from the East Coast of America in the 'Big Four' of Thrash Metal bands. By what name are they both known?

ANSWERS

1. Compass
2. Artificial snow
3. *Escherichia coli* (E.coli)
4. Electrons
5. Squid

6. Sulphuric acid
7. Wolf pack
8. Chocolate Agar
9. Angel's glow
10. Plague, pestilence
11. Insects
12. New Delhi, *Delhi Belly*
13. Radiation
14. Gold
15. Anthrax

2. BLISSFUL BIRDS

1. This bird has the largest bill compared to the size of its body. Interestingly, the bill is made up of Keratin in a latticework of hollow sections, like the insides of a sponge. When resting, the bird has to twist its head all the way around and rest its bill on its back. They mainly eat fruits but have been known to prey on insects and small lizards. Which bird is this that makes an appearance in many cartoons?

2. This bird, whose scientific name means 'Owl-face soft-feather', is the world's only flightless parrot. The bird evolved in far-flung islands of New Zealand, where there were no natural predators. Hence, over the course of time, they lost the ability to fly. The bird walks about the forest floor and uses its wings to it climb trees and then parachute to the floor. Being nocturnal in nature, its main defence mechanism is to freeze when startled so that it blends into the surroundings. Though these birds have a life expectancy of ninety years, due to habitat destruction and human-introduced predators

they are now a highly endangered species. What is this funny sounding name of this bird that the New Zealand government is trying to reintroduce into the wild?

3. These birds pee down their legs to cool down and to prevent bugs from crawling into their feathers. One of their key defensive mechanisms is to throw up on command. Since their diet mainly comprises of dead animals, the stink of the vomit is enough to drive away animals. They can also vomit on their young to keep predators away. A good way to dispose of rabid corpses is by feeding them to these birds, as they generally do not get not infected with rabies. It gets its name because of its bald head and dark plumage, which resembles that of a common domesticated bird. What is the name of this bird that enjoys federal protection under law?

4. These birds live in the deserts of the American southwest. They can fly but prefer the ground and can zip along through the desert at a blistering 32 km/hr. (For reference, Usain Bolt peaked at 44.7 km/hr during the final 100m sprint at the World Championships in Berlin on 16 August 2009.) The birds rarely run in a straight line and are so quick that they frequently catch rattlesnakes. They make a distinct long 'coo-coo' call; yet most people, when asked, would say that these birds go 'beep beep'. Which interesting bird is this, which has been immortalized, thanks to the television?

5. Eiji Nakatsu is a Japanese designer who set out to solve a certain issue that the world-famous bullet trains were facing. When the train entered a tunnel, a loud bang was heard due to the fixed air volume in the tunnel and the sudden increase in pressure from the entering train. Nakatsu studied a particular bird, especially the shape of its head, as he had noticed that when it dove for its prey, there were few ripples formed on the surface of the water. This is because the bird is the most efficient animal on earth to transition from low pressure (air) to high pressure (water). Consequently, they redesigned the nose of the train to eliminate the change in pressure and solved the problem. Which bird was hence responsible for the bullet trains' smooth journeys?

6. The hooded Pitohui (*Pitohui dichrous*), found in New Guinea, is a medium-sized songbird with a rich chestnut and black plumage. It eats certain beetles, which gives it a unique characteristic, and till this was observed in the Pitohui, only some very colourful frogs were known to have the same feature. This was discovered when scientists, preparing the birds' skins for display at museums, lost sensation in their hands. What is it that the hooded Pitohui has—in its skin and organs—that sets it apart from other birds?

7. The members of a certain community have made a pledge not to use Diclofenac, an anti-inflammatory

drug used to treat inflammatory diseases. This pledge was taken in order to ensure the continuity of a certain custom that required the participation of a certain bird of prey in the final rites. A study had shown that the presence of Diclofenac caused kidney failure in these birds when they ingested it from animals treated with the drug. Which community is this whose funeral rituals require the services of this bird and what bird is this?

8. Jahangir was a Mughal emperor who ruled during the early 1600s. He was an avid collector of art and a keen ornithologist, so he commissioned his court artist, Ustad Mansur, to paint a few of his favourite birds from the emperor's personal collection. This lovely painting is extremely important to scientists as it is anatomically correct and is the only known coloured depiction of the bird. Which bird is this that has become the symbol for the Durrel Zoo and is responsible for saving other animals from extinction?

9. This is the tallest bird in North America. Its name is made up of two words—one describes the sound it makes and the other describes the type of bird it is. Hunting and reduction of their wetland habitat had reduced their population to such an extent that in 1941, there were only twenty-three of them left. Today, there are over 700 of these birds, thanks largely to innovative breeding programmes. The sound they make is loud

enough to be heard several kilometers away. The same sound also gives its name to a childhood respiratory infection. Which endangered birds are these?

10. Migrating ducks and geese often use this aerodynamic principle to enable themselves to travel long distances, without getting tired. Each bird flies in the upwash of its neighbour's beating wings and this extra bit of supporting wind facilitates the lift, thereby saving energy; thus allowing them to cover huge distances in one go. What formation have we associated these birds with since we were kids?

11. The Anhinga is also known as the snake bird in reference to its long, thin neck, which has a snake-like appearance when it swims with its body submerged. But its common name results from its manner of procuring food, as it impales fishes with its thin, pointed beak. What is the name of this deft bird that should remind you of a game, which you'd usually see being played at parties?

12. The flutter you hear when a bird flies by is because of the turbulence created when air rushes over its wings. One bird has been able to overcome this problem—it has wings with serrated edges, which enables it to fly in absolute silence. This unique ability helps it hunt at night and adds to its already mystical reputation. Scientists and engineers are studying this bird to help design fans with blades that are noiseless. What bird

is this whose largest species has the very endearing scientific name *Bubo bubo*?

13. This wingless bird has heavy bones filled with marrow, a nostril at the tip of its nose (rather than on the beak like most birds), and cat-like whiskers to help navigate in the dark. It builds burrows like a badger and sleeps standing up. This has earned it the title of 'honorary mammals'. It is native to a certain country whose rugby team is named after the bird. Which bird is this that lays the largest egg in relation to its body size?

14. While these birds might stand out on land, in their natural environment their strange colour helps them stay hidden from predators and prey. Their black backs blend in with the darker colours below them so that they're difficult to spot from above. Their white chests help them blend in with the lighter, brighter surface colour as seen from below, pretty much rendering them near-invisible. In this species, the fattest and pudgiest males are the most desirable to the opposite sex, as after the egg is laid, it is the male who has to incubate it. What interesting birds are these, which can range from a size of 16 inches to 4 feet tall and are found exclusively in the Southern Hemisphere?

15. When India was choosing its national bird, Ornithologist Salim Ali favoured a lovely bird that is one of the heaviest flying birds in the world. Unfortunately, it lost to the peacock because its name could too easily be

mispronounced as a term of slander. With just about a couple of hundred birds left, this can become the first mega-species to go extinct in India after the loss of the cheetah. If Salim Ali had been successful, we might have been able to protect it better. Which magnificent but highly endangered bird is this?

ANSWERS

1. Toucan
2. Kakapo
3. Turkey Vulture
4. Roadrunner
5. Kingfisher
6. It is poisonous
7. Parsis; vultures
8. Dodo
9. Whooping Cranes
10. 'V' formation
11. Darter
12. Eurasian eagle-owl
13. Kiwi
14. Penguins
15. Great Indian Bustard

3. PACKED WITH PLANTS

1. Covering 70 lakh square kilometres and spreading over nine countries, this ecosystem represents half of the remaining green cover on earth. Every year, it absorbs 2.2 billion tons of carbon dioxide. One in ten known species in the world lives here. This constitutes the largest collection of living plants and animal species in the world. Scientists believe that less than 1 per cent of the flowering plant species there have been studied in detail for their medicinal potential. With it disappearing so rapidly, the continuity of this knowledge for the benefit of future generations is under threat. What is this vital resource, which is being destroyed at a relentless and foolish pace due to deforestation and forest fires?

2. These crops originally came from Peru, where the Aztec name for them meant 'plump thing with a navel'. These develop from the ovary at the base of the flower, and contain the seeds of the plant, which means that essentially they are fruits, though by popular definition

they are not. For a long time, Europeans thought it to be poisonous. Then, it was discovered that the harmful effects were caused by the juices interacting with the pewter plates they used. It still was a rarely used item till the Italians discovered its culinary attributes and spread it all over the world. What crop is this that caused so much confusion?

3. *Camellia sinensis* is an evergreen shrub, which is one of the most important plants in the history of civilization. The name *sinensis* means 'from China' in Latin. Different cultures use the product of the plant in different ways. The most popular variants one might come across are black, green, yellow and white. All these come from the same plant and get their characteristic colours only from the method of processing. What economically vital product does this plant provide?

4. This plant is a type of tall grass that was first mentioned in New Guinea in 8000 BC. Once other civilizations found out about its usefulness, the crop quickly spread. In 5 AD, an Indian chemist discovered a method to crystallize the main product from this plant and this led to the plant playing an important part in trade and economy. The majority of the stalk (up to three-quarters) is made of water, while up to 16 per cent is the compound that the chemist turned into the trade-worthy product, and the rest is fibre. The

worldwide production of this substance currently is 1.70 billion tonnes. What plant is this and what product is derived from it?

5. Researchers from the Slovak Academy of Sciences grew soya beans in a particular area to see how they would adapt to the conditions there. Compared to the plants grown in normal soil, the soya grown on a plot inside the area produced significantly different amounts of several dozens of protein. Among those were proteins that contribute to the production of seeds, as well as proteins involved in defending cells from heavy metal and radiation damage. They even discovered a protein, which is known to actually protect human blood from radiation. In which area did the scientists research?

6. The Belladonna plant's foliage and berries are extremely toxic when ingested. The plant, though, is of commercial importance as the drug 'Atropine', is obtained from it. The name 'belladonna' means 'beautiful woman' in Italian. The name refers to the fact that hundreds of years ago, the herb was used in eye-drops by women who wanted to appear seductive. Most visits to ophthalmologists begin with this drug. What purpose is it still used for?

7. *V. planifolia* is an orchid. It is native to Central America and grows in hot, wet tropical climates. A very popular product, with a unique flavour, is made from its fruits (resemble bananas) and are about 20 cm long. They are

mistakenly referred to as beans. It is so popular, in fact, that the flavour is most common amongst children, and it is the most highly stocked flavour. Every year, close to 900 tons of this product are produced. What is the popular genus name of this plant?

8. The Indian pipe plant, also known as the ghost plant, grows on fungi, which themselves grow on trees. It is one among a group of rare plants that lack a particular compound which we instantly associate with plants. Due to this unique feature, it is able to live in dense forests under thick trees. What does the Indian pipe plant lack?

9. *Helicoverpa* is a genus of moth that is a polyphagous and cosmopolitan pest species. The common term for the larva of this moth is 'budworm'. It attacks the fruiting bodies of certain crops, causing huge economic damage. In 1995, a certain entity was developed using strains of the bacterium *Bacillus thuringiensis* to combat this particular pest. This entity was given a name, which many people mistake it to be a reference to 'Biotechnology', but it is, in fact, a reference to the bacteria. What is the name of this entity, of which India is the largest grower, with almost 10 million hectares of this crop?

10. This plant from the ginger family is native to India. The ancient Harappan civilization initially used it as a dye, but they soon realized its culinary and medicinal

value. The rhizomes are boiled in water for about thirty to forty-five minutes and then dried in hot ovens, after which they are ground into a deep-orange-yellow powder. This is a natural source for curcuminoids, which are natural phenols that form a basis for many drug formulations. What is this powder, which has a warm, bitter flavour?

11. *Epipremnum aureum* is a flowering plant, which is native to islands in the Pacific. It is called by many names, one of them being 'Devil's vine', because it's almost impossible to kill as it stays green even if kept in complete darkness. It is genetically incapable of flowering and the last reported flower seen in one of these was in 1964. It has a particular name in India, thanks to a legend about a poverty-stricken farmer discovering this plant in his field and going on to become wealthy by growing and selling it. By what name do we know this plant in India?

12. This is a non-governmental organization, which promotes conservation, biodiversity, organic farming, rights of farmers and the process of seed saving. It has set up the largest direct marketing, fair trade organic network in the country. The name represents two things: India's collective source of food security being nine crops, and that seeds are the new gift of life. What is the name of this organization?

13. In the Blue Mountains of Eastern Oregon lives a

pathogenic fungus called 'Honey Mushroom' (*Armillaria ostoyae*). There is one single specimen, which is thought to be at least 2,000 years old and primarily lives beneath the ground and blooms in autumn. When it does, it covers 2,200 acres, spreading across almost 3.8 km. This leads it to hold what record title?

14. *Achras zapota* is a fruit plant we all know. It is grown for the fruit and the gum-like substance obtained from its latex and is mainly used for preparation of chewing gum. The name for the main compound required to make the gum comes from the local name for this fruit. The most popular chewing gum is also named after this compound. What fruit is this, which leaves a sweet taste and a sticky sensation in your mouth?

15. This plant from the *Rubiaceae* family is native to Africa. It is responsible for one of the most important export products of the continent. The particular species *arabica*, indigenous to Ethiopia, accounts for more than 70 per cent of the global production. There is a story that a certain Sheikh Omar, during exile, tried chewing berries from this plant but found them to be bitter. Roasting the seeds and chewing them did not help either. When he boiled them though, the resultant soup sustained him for days. He was apparently made a saint for this discovery. What is this soupy thing that is now one of the most sought after commodities in the world?

ANSWERS

1. The Amazon rainforest
2. Tomato
3. Tea
4. Sugarcane and sugar
5. Chernobyl
6. Dilating the pupils
7. Vanilla
8. Chlorophyll
9. Bt Cotton
10. Turmeric
11. Money Plant
12. Navdanya ('nine seeds' and 'new gift')
13. The largest single organism on earth
14. Sapota
15. Coffee

4. FANTASTIC FLOWERS AND TERRIFIC TREES

1. This plant was originally cultivated in what is present-day Turkey. Only in the sixteenth century was this plant brought into the country, which is strongly associated with it now. Its spread coincided with the Golden Age of that country and was soon seen as a symbol of the nation's culture. The curvaceous colourful flowers were omnipresent in paintings and other artwork. In the mid-seventeenth century, it became so popular that it created a 'mania', and bulbs of this flower were even used as currency. Till today, the plant and its flower are pretty much everywhere in this country. What country and plant are these?

2. This form of art is derived from an ancient Chinese horticultural practice, part of which was then redeveloped under the influence of Japanese Zen Buddhism. The skill lies in knowing when and how to trim the branches and restricting the root growth.

A common misconception is that these trees are a special species; in fact, any regular tree can be grown this way, though this is possible only with certain species of trees that have the ability to adapt to different environments. What form of art is this?

3. According to a popular author, in the language used during the Victorian era, certain meanings were attached to two flowers after which two sisters are named in her seminal work. The elder sister is named after a flower that is susceptible to damage, is best grown in a basket and has to be sheltered from wind and excess light. It also harbours the meaning of 'resentment and anger'. The younger sister signifies 'beauty, elegance, sweetness' and the flower associated with her means 'remembered beyond the tomb'. What are these two flowers, what is the name of the younger sister and the series?

4. The Rafflesia is a genus of parasitic flowering plants discovered in the 1800s in Indonesia, which has no stems, leaves or true roots. The only part of the plant that can be seen outside the host vine is the five-petalled flower, which can grow up to 3 feet across and weigh 10 kg, making it the largest single flower in the world. It is unique as it is also the only land plant without a gene for chloroplasts. One other thing that sets it apart is its smell, which is meant to attract flies for pollination. What smell does it have?

5. *Butea monosperma* is a deciduous tree, which is commonly found across India and known for its bright orange-red flowers. Rabindranath Tagore, in his poems, used it to refer to spring. Santiniketan, where he lived, had an abundance of these trees. The tree lent its Bengali name (*pôlash*) to the town of Palashi and the anglicized version of that has been immortalized in a historic incident that happened there. The common name for the tree comes from the vivid imagery it conjures when in full bloom. What is the common name for this tree and what is the historical incident that gets its name from this tree?

6. In horticulture, this term means 'falling off at maturity' and 'tending to fall off', in reference to trees and shrubs that seasonally shed leaves, usually in autumn. In medical terminology, it relates to body parts that fall off and are replaced by new ones, for example, a child's or a young animal's first set of teeth. Italians in mountainous regions use the Latin adjective version of the word to refer to shooting stars. What is this word?

7. Many of the buildings in this city were built on foundations of tree trunks, and 1,200 years later, the same trunks still support them. They will stay there for thousands of years more—as long as they stay submerged. Since they are not exposed to oxygen, they do not rot. Some have actually started to petrify due to the mineral rich water. In another thousand years, they

will actually become stone pilings. In which city is this?

8. *Prunus serrulata* is a type of tree found in the temperate zone that produces a pink flower, which is the national flower of Japan. The tree is cultivated purely for ornamental use. Though it shares its name and genes with a popular fruit, the tree does not produce any fruit at all. One of the most ancient practices is 'Hanami', which started in 700 AD that literally means picnicking under this tree. Hanami festivals are celebrated throughout Japan and attract millions of visitors all through the period of bloom. What tree is this that has been a part of Japanese art for centuries?

9. This movement started in 1974 under the leadership of Gaura Devi who was the head of the Mahila Mangal Dal, at Reni village. The day the lumbermen were to cut the trees, Gaura Devi led twenty-seven women to confront them and eventually prevented the felling of trees. Soon, this became a movement across the state. What did the women do, and consequently, by what name is the movement known?

10. Thimmamma Marrimanu is in Kadiri, Andhra Pradesh. Legend has it that Thimmamma was the wife of a Bala Veerayya who died in 1434 by committing sati. Marrimanu is said to have sprung up at that place. It is in the *Guinness Book of World Records* for covering an area of 4.7 acres. What is Thimmamma Marrimanu?

11. This tree is endemic to the island archipelago nation of Seychelles and the unique shape of its huge seed has led to many myths and legends. Its scientific name is *Lodoicea callipyge* in which 'Callipyge' is Greek for 'beautiful buttocks', which is a description of the shape of the seed. For a long time, sailors who found the seeds thought they were from a strange tree growing under the Indian Ocean. Only after the 1600s, when these islands were properly explored, were these trees discovered and the myth of the underwater tree was broken. By what common name are these trees known, thanks to their location and the type of tree they are?

12. *Paubrasilia echinata* is a timber tree, commonly known as the _____ wood tree. This plant has dense, orange-red heartwood that shines brightly and its premier wood is used to make bows for stringed instruments. During the early 1500s, the Portuguese laid claim to a large expanse of land in South America, where this tree was found. The wood and the deep red dye obtained from the tree were in high demand in the European cloth industry. In fact, it was so vital that the land came to be known as 'Terra do X' (land of X). We now know it simply as 'X'. What country is this whose national tree is the *P. echinata*?

13. The Tambalacoque tree is endemic to Mauritius and has been flowering for thousands of years. But over the last 300 years, the population has steadily declined.

One theory attributes it to the loss of a particular animal from the same area. This theory got stronger when it was discovered that when fruits of this tree were force-fed to turkeys, the resulting seeds, collected from the droppings, germinated. Which animal is supposed to be linked to the decline of this tree?

14. Barbados is an island country in the West Indies that supposedly gets its name from 'Los Barbados', which means 'the _____ ones'. This is believed to refer to the long, hanging roots of the *Ficuscitrifolia* or the '_____ fig tree', which is indigenous to the island. The name refers to how these trees look when their roots are fully-grown. What are these trees known as which led to the name of this island?

15. *Adenium obesum* is a flowering plant that is native to Africa. It is known for its extremely colourful flowers. It also has a thick caudice (stem), which helps it to grow in arid regions where water is scarce. Due to these characteristics, it has a certain common name. When searching for this name online, the first results you get will be of a hit song about 'lost love and longing' by British musician, Sting, from his 1999 album *Brand New Day*. How do we better know *A. obesum*?

ANSWERS

1. Holland; Tulips
2. Bonsai
3. Petunia and Lily; Lily is the younger sister; *Harry Potter* is the name of the series.
4. Rotting Flesh, hence known as the 'corpse flower'
5. Flame of the Forest, Battle of Plassey
6. Deciduous
7. Venice
8. East Asian Cherry
9. They hugged the trees and didn't let go. 'Chipko (to hug) Movement'
10. It is a banyan tree and it is the largest in the world.
11. Sea Coconut or 'Coco de Mer'
12. Brazil
13. The Dodo
14. Bearded fig tree
15. 'Desert Rose'

5. BEASTS IN BOOKS

1. *The Sheep-_____* is a 1983 book by Dick King-Smith set in rural England. The writer had been a farmer for about twenty years and based many of his books on his experiences. This particular book tells the story of a certain animal that the farmer wins, which then takes on the role of a completely different animal after being adopted by the farmer's dog. What was the name of this animal (which became famous after a movie adaptation by the same name) and what kind of animal was he (fill in the blank in the title)?

2. In his classic children's book *The Trumpet of the _____*, E.B. White tells the story of Louis, who is born mute and whose parents despaired of him never being able to communicate. He goes to school to learn to read and write, but this doesn't help him win the love of his life. Then, his father steals a trumpet for him and he becomes a sensation—a world-famous musician. What kind of animal is the protagonist of this book? The title of the book is a pun on its particular species.

3. This 1923 book by the Austrian author Felix Salten is titled _____, *a Life in the Woods* and tells the story of an animal, brought up by his mother, in a forest. The story traces his life from that of a baby to an adult, dealing with a variety of learning experiences, especially the most important lesson of all—that humans are dangerous! The book was translated into English in 1928, and it was turned into a famous movie in 1942. What is the name of the title character and what kind of animal is he in the book?

4. Judith Kerr was a beloved writer and illustrator of children's books and one of her most famous books is *The _____ Who Came to Tea*. Given that Kerr and her family had fled from Nazi Germany, many adult readers and critics often wondered if the events and, title character in the book were metaphors for Nazis or Nazism. When asked, Kerr replied, patiently and slowly, 'It is the story of a _____ who came to tea.' What greedy animal did Kerr write about?

5. In Rudyard Kipling's delightful *Just So Stories*, the story of *The _____'s Child* is a humorous story about how a certain animal got its characteristic feature. It tells the tale of a young animal whose insatiable curiosity about what a crocodile has for dinner leads him right to the Limpopo river where the crocodile lives. When the crocodile tries to eat him for dinner, the young animal, with the help of a python, pulls

away from the crocodile, leading to a certain part of his body being stretched out. What is the title of the story and, therefore, what kind of animal was this curious youngster?

6. In the *Harry Potter* series, Harry's pet, Hedwig, is as beloved to readers as any other character in the books or movies. Indeed, Hedwig is indispensable to Harry, carrying his letters to and fro and bringing him parcels from all his friends whenever he has to spend his summer holidays holed up at home with his dreadful uncle, aunt and cousin. Introduced to us quite early in the very first book, what kind of animal is Hedwig?

7. This character in Rudyard Kipling's famous *Jungle Book* is the leader of his pack and one of the mentors of Mowgli, the human they adopt. What kind of animal is he and what is his name, which, quite fittingly, in Hindi or Urdu, means 'lone'?

8. *A _____ in Times Square* is an award-winning children's book by George Selden, and tells the story of Chester, a young animal from Connecticut who lands up in Times Square, New York. He makes friends with a family who run a newsstand there. Along with a cat and a mouse, who also live in the newsstand, he explores the city and, in the course of the story, reveals his great talent for making music, being able to reproduce all manners of great songs and tunes! What

kind of animal is Chester (fill in the blanks in the title)?

9. Lewis Carroll's masterpiece, *Alice in Wonderland*, had many interesting and intriguing animals gambolling through its pages. Alice meets a dormouse, a Cheshire cat, a Dodo and many, many others. However, most of these animals are independent and she meets them in social settings or as she wanders about. What animals does she see being used by the Queen of Hearts to play a game of croquet? One particular animal is wielded as the mallet (the small hammer) while the other animal serves as the ball.

10. In a Ruskin Bond story called *A _____ for all Seasons*, we see the world and the foolishness of human actions through the eyes of Speedy, who is a very clever animal. Speedy's wry utterances and observations make up the story and no one can deny how smart his entire species is! After all, videos on the Internet have shown that they use traffic signals to cross the roads, while a popular folktale talks about how they use available resources to access tiny amounts of water. What kind of animal is Speedy, seen increasingly in many Indian cities?

The next four questions are from the Roald Dahl classic, *James and the Giant Peach*, where seven-year-old James Henry Trotter escapes from his wicked aunts and hides inside a Giant Peach, with seven other companions from his aunts' garden. Based on the descriptions below, can you identify five of these companions?

11. The oldest and wisest of James's companions is a wonderful musician who eventually joins the New York Symphony Orchestra.

12. This character is exuberant and is always announcing, in delighted tones, that he is a PEST! He is a bit of a rascal and his biggest boast is that he has a hundred feet, although the number is really only forty-two!

13. The third companion is smooth all over and blind and is disdainful of the Pest's pride in being a Pest! He himself is proud of the fact that he is a farmer's friend and claims that every grain of soil in a field passes through him and others like him.

14. Finally, two key characters who help the company out of much danger are two different animals that can produce thread and, when the story ends, both of them set up a factory weaving ropes for tightrope walkers.

15. Terry Pratchett's famous Discworld is a flat world that floats through space, carried on the backs of four giant elephants. However, the elephants themselves stand on the back of a massive _____, called the Great A'Tuin, who moves through space with the entire world on its back. What kind of animal is the Great A'Tuin, whose origins can be traced to myths from across the world?

ANSWERS

1. *Pig*; Babe
2. *Swan*, Louis is a Trumpeter Swan
3. Bambi; a roe deer.
4. A tiger
5. *The Elephant's Child*, an elephant
6. A snowy owl
7. A wolf; Akela
8. A cricket; *Cricket*
9. A flamingo (mallet) and a hedgehog (ball)
10. A crow
11. A grasshopper
12. A centipede
13. An earthworm
14. A spider and a silkworm
15. A turtle

6. MEMORABLE MAMMALS

1. These animals found in South America are known only in the domesticated state and there are no known wild variants. They are not ruminants but have three stomach compartments that allow them to consume lower quality, high cellulose foods, which are usually found in places they inhabit at high attitudes. One of the most characteristic behaviours of these animals is its ability to spit when angry. Depending on how angry they are, they can reach further back into the stomach and spit out more food. This is referred to in a humorous instance in a Tintin book, where Captain Haddock gets into a spitting fight with one of these animals. What delightful sounding animals are these?

2. These mammals have a unique form of social justice (thereby proving that the concept is not exclusive to human beings). These animals drink half their weight in blood from cattle and horses every day. If one of them goes hungry, another will regurgitate blood for

the friend. If one hungry member goes to another and that animal refuses to help, the rest of the colony punishes the selfish member by not giving it food. Which species, named after a mythical creature, has this interesting system of justice?

3. The Reindeer is a type of deer that is found in cold regions. The species has a rare trait: both males and females have antlers. Male reindeer use their antlers to compete with each other during the mating season and lose the antlers in autumn. They only get new antlers the following summer. A female reindeer, though, retain their antlers throughout winter and the following year, until they calve. How would this fact upset a now-popular Christmas tradition?

4. The scientific name of this animal is *Boselaphustrago camelus*. This translates into the very confusing 'cow-horse goat-camel'. The common name comes from the fusion of the local words for a colour it can take on and the type of animal it is. What is the common name for this large Asian antelope?

5. This beautiful animal has been revealed to be genetically linked to the tiger, but gets its name from another big cat. It is estimated that only around 7,000 of these animals remain. They have thick fur and wide paws to distribute their weight evenly and long tails that help them jump gracefully between rocky crevices. Unlike other big cats, this cat cannot roar and only hisses and

mews. What lovely animal is this that can be seen in the Indian Himalayas?

6. There are seven tiger subspecies and their scientific names mostly all refer to their geographical area of incidence, for example, *amoyensis* (Amoy), *balinicus* (Bali), *sumatraensis* (Sumatra), etc. Only one subspecies has a scientific name that honours an individual—the Indochinese tiger. To whom is the name dedicated?

7. The Salvador/Warts pathway in biochemistry is also known as the 'X Pathway', and it controls organ size in animals through the regulation of cell proliferation and apoptosis. The pathway gets its name from one of its key signaling components—the protein kinase 'X'. Mutations in this gene lead to tissue overgrowth or an X-like phenotype. X is the short form of the name of an animal, whose name comes from the ancient Greek words 'river horse'. What is X, which is fitting considering the features it leads to?

8. The common name for these mammals from the family 'Manidae' comes from the Malay word for 'something that rolls up'. They are the only known mammals to have protective keratin scales that cover their skin. These serve as defense against bigger predators, but unfortunately cannot help them against their greatest threat, that is poaching by humans. These animals are highly endangered, as they are the most trafficked in the world because of their meat and scales due to

extreme loss of habitat. What unfortunate animals are these?

9. This animal was not known to the world till 1869, when the skin of one was studied with great interest. As of now, there are only 1,864 of these beautiful animals in the wild and another 266 in captivity. Every single one of them is from only one country. They have lived on earth for millions of years but were almost wiped out by humans in the last few decades. Unanimously described as 'cute', the collective noun for a group of these animals is 'an embarrassment of _____'. What animal is this that adorns the logo for one of the biggest wildlife organizations in the world?

10. 12,000 years ago, these animals spread all over South East Asia. Today, there about a 100,000 of them on just two islands. They are the only ones of their kind in Asia; all their cousins are from Africa. They are extremely smart and have been observed making and using tools in the wild, with one specimen recently observed engaging in the very human activity of spear fishing. Their homes are currently being demolished at a frantic pace to make way for palm trees, as palm oil has become a major item of export. What uniquely coloured gentle giants are these, also referred to as the 'grand old man of the forest'?

11. This is one of the very few mammals that are venomous. It hunts by tracking electrical signals like a shark.

Because it has no teeth, it uses gravel to break down food like a bird, and it doesn't have a stomach but has a gullet that connects directly to the intestine. When it was first discovered and taken for classification, the scientists thought it was a prank played on them. When its DNA was decoded in 2008, scientists were astounded to see that it shared genes with reptiles, birds and mammals. What is this disorienting animal, which became even more popular, thanks to a children's TV series, featuring one as a secret agent?

12. These animals are apex predators as there is no known animal that preys on them, but they are on the endangered list purely because of prey depletion, loss of habitat of and pollution—all caused by humans. They have a two-part name, both of which are misnomers. Experts have hypothesized that the current name is an unfortunate mistranslation of a Spanish name, *asesina-ballenas*, where they got the order of the words wrong. In 2019, a new species of this animal called 'Type D' was discovered at the tip of South America. What is the name of this species, which makes them sound like villains?

13. These animals have a very complex social structure and because they reproduce slowly, the removal of even a few individuals from a troop can catastrophically impact its ability to sustain itself. Around 110,000 are left on the planet. From habitat loss to rapidly growing

human habitation are the biggest threats they face. The most famous of the species has a very interesting scientific name. It's the only one where it's the same word twice and that word, too, is its common name. What is the scientific name of this wonderful creature, which can weigh up to 200 kg and is our closest cousin evolutionarily?

14. This species split from its more prevalent cousin about forty million years ago and took residence in the area above 60° North Latitude. The area they mainly inhabit gets its name from the Greek word for the animal, and the antipodal region gets its name from the fact that this animal does not exist there. Currently numbering around 20,000, they are dwindling fast due to climate change, as they need hard, strong ice to carry their weight. What animals are these?

15. These marsupials are among the smallest mammals in the world, small enough to wrap themselves around an adult human's thumb! They can weigh between 10 grams to 45 grams and are nocturnal beings, eating nectar and pollen from eucalyptus, bottle brushes and banksias. Many species have prehensile tails, allowing them to hang from branches. Despite their tiny size and the numerous predators they have to hide from, their most dangerous enemy might just be the human being, who are destroying their habitats. What are these endearing little animals known as?

ANSWERS

1. Llama
2. Vampire Bat
3. Rudolph, the red-nosed reindeer, should either be a 'she' or be depicted without antlers
4. Nilgai
5. Snow Leopard
6. Jim Corbett, *Panthera tigris corbetti*
7. Hippo
8. Pangolins
9. The Giant Panda
10. Orangutans
11. Duck-billed Platypus
12. Killer Whales
13. *Gorilla gorilla*
14. Polar Bear
15. Pygmy Possum

7. ROCKING REPTILES AND ASTONISHING AMPHIBIANS

1. This particular species was discovered in the early 2000s in Kerala. Since then, it has fascinated herpetologists from around the world, who argue that it should be called a 'living fossil' since its roots date back over seventy million years, to a time when dinosaurs still walked the earth! Interestingly, this frog may have survived four mass extinctions! Given that its closest relative was found in Seychelles recently, this frog may also help prove the Gondwanaland theory. It lives underground and comes out only once a year to breed. What is the name of this frog, which is a reference to the bright 'royal' colour of its skin?

2. Scientists have found that a characteristic change that this animal undergoes is not actually related to its surroundings, but seems to be related to its mood! What is this moody reptile that has an amazing ability to rotate both its eyes independently?

3. Zond-5 was a Russian lunar mission that sent a number of living creatures to orbit around the moon. These were, technically, the first earthlings to orbit the moon! Apart from seeds, bacteria, worms and fruit flies, the spacecraft also carried two larger reptiles, which survived the journey and returned to earth, though they showed a 10 per cent loss in body weight, something that is now seen in any astronaut going to space. What were these two placid creatures?

4. Despite the bad rap that snakes have, just about 2 per cent of all snakes are actually venomous! However, there is one continent on earth where venomous snakes outnumber the non-venomous ones. Where is this?

5. These snakes from the viper family have a particular name because of the presence of a special heat-sensing organ called a 'Loreal ___' located between the eye and the nostril on both sides of their heads. These help the snake detect warm-blooded preys, such as birds and rodents, in the dark. This feature gives the snake its name and not, as sometimes mistakenly thought, the type of place where one would find this snake. What is the common name for the *Crotalinae* sub-family of vipers?

6. The females of these lizards have an incredible ability called facultative-parthenogenesis, which allows them

to breed without the involvement of any male lizards at all. Despite having only a mother, the offspring are not clones, as the mother's half-set of chromosomes doubles up. Hence, it is not a duplicate of her genome. These lizards are also venomous. They are the largest living species of lizards, growing up to a length of 10 feet and weighing up to 70 kg. What lizards are these, which get their names from the island in Indonesia where they were discovered first?

7. The *palustris* crocodile is one of three species found in India. They are medium-sized, growing up to 10 feet in both sexes and are found in freshwater. They have a very broad snout and feed on fish and small mammals. Their common name comes from a word in Hindi related to 'corruption' and has no connection to its English word that might lead you to think that these animals have certain villainous characteristics. What is the common name of these crocodiles?

8. This snake is the longest venomous snake in the world and is among the deadliest ones known. Its name refers to its cannibalistic tendencies, and the second part of its scientific name, despite popular legends, does not refer to the wife of the man who first described this snake! What is the common name for this snake?

9. *Python regius* is the smallest species of python and is found in Africa. It is also one of the species of

snakes kept as pets due to its docile nature. One of its common names is the Royal Python, because it was believed to have been worn by Cleopatra as jewellery. Its other common name comes from the characteristic position it gets into when threatened. What is name of this python?

10. *Micrixalus* are a genus of endangered frogs that are endemic to the Western Ghats in India. They have peculiar mating and territory protecting rituals, which lent them their common name. The male frogs call from a spot close to running water. They then tap their hind feet and extend one foot outwards and shake it. This behaviour called 'foot flagging' and is done with either leg. What interesting name is given to these frogs because of this characteristic behaviour that makes them sound like they are having a jolly good time?

11. This particular reptile has a phenomenally specialized body that helps it eat its favourite spherical food. Despite these objects being much larger than the animal's head, its elastic body allows it to swallow these objects whole. It then forces the object down its body, and its protruding spine along its vertebral column is used to crack open the object so its contents are released. The remainder is then spat out. What is the general, and pretty easily descriptive, name given to this creature?

12. This particular dinosaur was bipedal and fossils have shown that it had strange protrusions over its eyes. Explanations range from these being different for males and females to these enhancing their sense of smell. Theirs were among the earliest dinosaur fossils to be discovered and very plentiful. At the time they were discovered, they were the only known dinosaurs to have had vertebrae that were concave on two sides. This led to them being named 'Strange Lizard'. What is the generic name of this dinosaur, whose pronunciation sounds like a French person answering a phone call?

13. This tiny chameleon is one among four miniaturized leaf chameleon species discovered by researchers in Madagascar. However, it is quite sad that all of these species are already at risk due to human activities. One of them is called *Brookesia tristis*, which translates into 'Sad leaf chameleon', alluding to its endangered status. What is the common name of the most critically endangered of these species (*Brookesia desperate*), facing threats from various human activities such as aquaculture, mining and quarrying?

14. The X is the legendary king of serpents, which is born from a snake egg hatched under a hen. It is supposed to be highly venomous and can kill a person just by staring at them. It makes an appearance in a variety of movies and TV shows and the most popular one plays a very important role in a children's book franchise.

The plant 'Y' is known as the King of Herbs and legend has it that it is the only antidote to X venom. What is this feared villainous animal and the popular herb, both of which get their names from the Greek word for 'Kingly'?

15. This highly endangered freshwater crocodile has a long narrow snout lined with teeth. Males develop a little bump on the edge of their snout, which has been compared to a pot. The name of this animal is directly derived from the local word for this pot. What is the name of this unusual little predator, which is facing extinction due to human activities?

ANSWERS
1. Purple frog
2. Chameleon
3. Steppe tortoises
4. Australia, of course!
5. Pit vipers
6. Komodo dragon
7. Mugger crocodile
8. King cobra; the scientific name is *Ophiophagus hannah*
9. Ball python
10. Dancing frogs
11. The egg-eating snake

12. Allosaurus
13. Desperate leaf chameleon
14. the basilisk and basil
15. The gharial

8. INTERESTING INSECTS

1. These insects have been around for more than 300 million years and are some of the most expert fliers known. They can move straight up or down, fly backwards, stop and hover, make hairpin turns at full speed (48 km/h) or in slow motion, and even mate in mid-air. They would starve if they couldn't fly, because they only eat prey they catch while flying. One of the most interesting features is that they breathe through their bottoms. What is this interesting insect?

2. These insects get their name from the waste matter that they consume. They are found in a variety of habitats and, as is often recounted, on every continent except Antarctica. These insects need to move in a straight line once they've got their food. In the daytime, they use polarized light around the sun. What unique ability, in the entire animal kingdom, do some species display at night, to navigate in a straight line and what is the general name these insects are known by?

3. This insect, often thought to be a lucky insect, is known in English by a name that connects it to the Virgin Mary (Jesus's mother). In India, in some languages, the name of this insect translates to 'Indra's cowherd'. What is this pretty insect that is widely popular for eating pests, hence beloved by gardeners around the world, and is the name of a popular English publisher of children's books?

4. The *Acanthaspis petax* is an insect found in Africa that preys on ants, beetles and flies. It has a peculiar characteristic of taking the carcass of its favourite prey and wearing it on its body to disguise itself when it stalks the prey. This incredible feature gives the bug a name that makes it sound like it's from a Jason Bourne movie. By what name, which refers to an act of killing prompted by political or religious motives, is this bug known?

5. It is a well-known fact that this insect is listed as the most dangerous animal in the world! What is this deadly insect, which has killed more humans (estimated to be in billions) than any other animal in history (yes, even more than other humans!)?

6. Silverfish are small wingless insects, which gets their name from their colour and the way they move. The scientific name *L. saccharina* refers to the fact that their diet primarily consists of carbohydrates such as starch and sugar. This is the reason they are usually

found in a particular place in our houses. This gives rise to this insect being referred to by a two-word term; the first word referring to the thing it supposedly feeds off and the second word referring to the type of animal it is. This is a misnomer, as silverfish are insects and the type of animal mentioned is usually found in the soil. By what erroneous name are silverfish referred to?

7. These insects construct mounds with amazing architectural feats complete with arches, tunnels, chimneys, insulation and nursery chambers. The mounds are always aligned north to south, to minimize exposure to the sun and thereby control the ambient temperature inside. Due to the almost compass-like nature of the mounds, what name has been given to the animals that build these?

8. These insects are (as of 2019) the loudest known creatures in the insect world. Their 'song' can hit 100 decibels or more (for reference, that's the sound of an approaching train or a nightclub, and can cause hearing loss in humans in five minutes!). Different species hit different volumes and scientists believe their volume is correlated with their body size. What deafening insects are these that we usually associate with summer evenings and 'chirps'?

9. *Ophiocordyceps unilateralis* is a fungus found in tropical rainforests that can infect a certain species

of ants. Once infected, the ant changes behaviour completely. It leaves the nest and heads to an area suitable for fungal growth, where it attaches itself to the vein of a plant. After about four to ten days, the fungus grows out of the ant's head and releases its spores. Due to the change in behaviour of these ants, a certain term is given to them that makes them sound like characters from a horror film. By what name are these infected ants known, because they resemble a corpse being controlled by witchcraft?

10. This species of insect is found in many parts of the world. But the North American species is famous for its annual migration over 3,000 kilometres to forests in Central America and Mexico. These insects fly in large numbers, often returning to the same spot they'd visited the previous year. Although they look ridiculously light, they alight on the trees in such large numbers that they may cause branches to collapse! What are these colourful insects, whose numbers are threatened by logging or tree cutting in Mexican forests?

11. Research has shown that a certain toxin, called melittin, may be able to kill the Human Immunodeficiency Virus (HIV) while leaving other cells intact. This toxin is found in the venom of a certain insect. Researchers are also exploring the use of this venom in alleviating pain in those suffering from rheumatoid arthritis.

Which insect's venom is this, whose components may prove highly beneficial to humans (though the act of transmitting it naturally is rather fatal to the insect)?

12. This insect may look harmless, but it can release a boiling, explosive mixture of the chemicals, hydroquinone and hydrogen peroxide, in a fine spray that can reach temperatures of 100°Celsius! These chemicals are stored in compartments within its own body so that they don't mingle and explode *inside*! Some species can direct this spray with stunning accuracy. What beetle is this, whose name may remind you of a certain aircraft?

13. It is well-known that fireflies (which are neither flies nor produce fire!) are bioluminescent and communicate through flashes of light. They are also amazingly energy-efficient in producing this light, which also attracts preys. How early in its life cycle does a firefly start producing light?

14. This animal is often used as an important example of natural selection as its characteristic features evolved in a relatively short span of time, proving the theory of survival of the fittest. The initial characteristic of this species were that they were white, speckled with black dots, to allow them camouflage with the white, lichen-covered bark of the trees they were on. However, as industrial pollution set in, in the nineteenth century, the tree barks turned dark and sooty. There was a rise

in the number of specimens with melanism (or dark colouring), allowing them to hide against the darker trees. This then became the predominant population. However, when a pollution-control programme was introduced in the twentieth century, the tree trunks became cleaner and the darker moths became more visible to the prey, and thus there was a resurgence of the white-winged species. What amazing insect is this?

15. Fill in the blanks with the name of an insect to complete this witty poem by Ogden Nash.

The ___ has made himself illustrious
Through constant industry industrious.
So what?
Would you be calm and placid
If you were full of formic acid?

ANSWERS

1. Dragonflies
2. Dung beetles. They navigate using the Milky Way.
3. Ladybird (from 'Our Lady', a name used to refer to the Virgin Mary); in India, it is known as 'Indragopa' in some places.
4. Assassin bug
5. Mosquitoes
6. Bookworms
7. Magnetic termites

8. Cicadas
9. Zombie ant
10. Monarch butterflies
11. Honeybee
12. Bombardier beetle
13. From the egg upwards! Their eggs can produce a faint glow.
14. The peppered moth
15. Ant

9. MAGNIFICENT MARINE LIFE

1. The Chinese used to rear these fishes in their ponds. Whenever they had guests, they would keep these fishes temporarily in smaller vessels, allowing the guests to see them from all sides. This traditional temporary Chinese display, over the years, led to the unfortunate practice of housing these fishes permanently in these vessels. This has been proven to be detrimental to the fish's health and in some places such as Rome, the practice has been banned on grounds of animal cruelty. Which fish is this and what is the vessel it is usually kept it?

2. Unlike other bony fishes, these do not have swim bladders. Hence they have to keep swimming all the time, even when they are asleep. Otherwise, they will sink to the ocean floor. This is one of the reasons why, unfortunately, a huge number of these already endangered fishes are lost, because they keep getting caught in nets. What fishes are these that have extremely streamlined bodies that help them move stealthily?

3. The fish from the Diodontidae family can reach a diameter of up to 35 inches (90 cm). It puffs up in size by swallowing water and storing it in its stomach. If the fish is taken out of the water, it can inflate in a similar way by swallowing air. It gets its name from a defence mechanism by which it radiates sharp spines outwards when the fish inflates itself. What is the name of the fish, which also refers to a land animal with spines?

4. These animals are what are known as molluscs. They are 'filter feeders', and it has been shown that a well-stocked bed of these can filter and clean a marine system in just weeks. What is unique about these animals is that they can change gender from male to female and back again depending on which is best for mating at that time. They become intrinsically valuable when they get irritated by any object that gets caught inside them. What animal is this?

5. This freshwater fish can live out of water for several years. It secretes a mucus cocoon and burrows itself under the unbaked earth. It takes in air through a built-in breathing tube that leads to the surface. It has both gills and an organ that is usually not found in fishes. It is the oldest species of jawed, bony fishes that are still extant. The name of the fish comes from the fact that it has this special organ. What is the name of this fish that can live upto the age of sixty-five?

6. In 2010, a new species of mushroom was found in Malaysia. It produces sponge-like rubbery orange fruit bodies. Scientists were fascinated by its spongy appearance so much so that they couldn't help themselves and named it after everyone's favorite resident of a place named after a hot fashion statement. They named it *Spongiforma*_____*ii*. What is the name of the species that kids should recognize?

7. The fishes from the genus Hippoglossus are all large flatfish that swim along the sea floor on one side of the body with both eyes on the upper side. They used to be especially popular as a delicacy on Catholic holy days. This led to them being referred to by a certain name. The name comes from two words that mean 'holy' and 'flat fish'. By what name are these fishes commonly known?

8. This animal makes an appearance in several children's stories and even a song by The Beatles, but what you may not know is that it has three hearts, which pump blue-coloured blood. Most of these animals are thought to have some venom, which comes from bacteria living in them. They are extremely intelligent and are capable of learning from experience and have been observed using tools. Which animal is this that can blend seamlessly into its background?

9. The Sea Cow and the Dugong are highly endangered marine herbivorous mammals. They belong to a

certain order of animals named because of an apparent resemblance to a group of beings in Greek mythology. These dangerous creatures lured sailors with their voices to be shipwrecked along their island. We use the same word today to mean an audible alarm (like their voices). What is the name of the order?

10. *Turritopsis dohrnii* is a small species of jellyfish found in the Mediterranean Sea. They have the unique capability to revert to a sexually immature stage after having reached maturity as an individual. They begin their lives as free-swimming larvae and then settle down as a colony of polyps. These then bud off and become jellyfishes, and when they become sick or grow old, they revert to the polyp form and go through the cycle again. Theoretically, this cycle can go on indefinitely, which leads to this jellyfish's common name. By what name is this jellyfish known, which makes it sound like a supervillain?

11. The Exocet is a French anti-ship missile, which is launched from underwater and takes a low trajectory, skimming the surface, before striking its targets. It is named after Exocoetidae, which are a family of marine fish that have long fins that enable them to do something that fish normally cannot do. They evolved to do this to escape from predators like dolphins and tuna. What are these fishes known as?

12. This popular animal has acute eyesight in and out of

water and can hear frequencies ten times the upper limit of humans. However, it has no sense of smell and relies on sonar for hunting. An interesting trait this animal has is an ability to shut off half its brain while sleeping, ensuring at all times that the other half is working. It also has two stomachs—one for storing food and the other to carry out digestion. What delightful animal is this?

13. This is a type of fish that looks like an eel and is the only known animal to have a skull but no vertebral column. They are known for the copious amounts of slime they produce when threatened. They also have the amazing ability to absorb the nutrients they need to survive through their skin while swimming in putrid waters near animal corpses. Their name might remind you of an English word that refers to old women, especially witches. What is the name by which these slimy fishes are known?

14. The largest fish in the world can grow up to a whopping 45 feet and weigh 30 tonnes! As huge as this fish is and however villainous its relatives are considered to be, this family is actually very gentle and feeds on nothing bigger than plankton. Its misleading name is just a description of its size and not its actual biological description. Found in Gujarat and Lakshadweep, it is unfortunately in the endangered list due to the impact of overfishing and vessel strikes. What majestic fish is this?

15. The Anableps inhabit freshwaters in South America. They spend most of their time on the surface of the water. Their diet consists of both terrestrial insects and small fishes. They have specially evolved eyes that are positioned on the top of their heads. Their unique characteristic is an eye that has two pupils, which are divided by a layer of tissue. The thickness of the lens changes from top to bottom to account for the difference in refractive indices between air and water. The upper half is adapted for vision when in air and the lower half for vision when in water. Owing to this amazing feature, what is the common name of this fish?

ANSWERS
1. Goldfish in glass bowls
2. Sharks
3. Porcupine fish
4. Oyster
5. Lungfish
6. *Spongiforma squarepantsii* (named after the cartoon character Spongebob Squarepants)
7. Halibut
8. Octopus
9. Sirenia (after the Greek 'sirens')
10. Immortal jellyfish

11. Flying fish
12. Dolphin
13. Hagfish
14. Whale shark
15. The four-eyed fish

10. SUPERLATIVE SPECIMENS

1. A cheetah can reach up to 120 km/hr in short bursts, but it is nowhere close to being the fastest member of the animal kingdom. That title belongs to a particular bird of prey that has a characteristic high-speed dive when hunting for prey. They were known to reach 300 km/hr; then, one was recorded diving at a record 389 km/hr. When these birds pull out of these hyper-dives after clutching their prey, they undergo 27Gs of deceleration. Compare this to the 4Gs that astronauts face during take-off and the maximum of 8Gs astronauts face on a ballistic reentry, at which point most normal humans would pass out. Which bird is this with such amazing speeds?

2. *Lineus longissimus,* also known as the bootlace worm, is commonly found along the coasts of Britain. It is usually about 5 to 10 millimetres in width. In 1864, one specimen was washed ashore in Scotland after a storm, and it was measured to be 55 m (approx. 180 feet) long. This puts it firmly as number one in a particular

list, which is usually attributed to either a whale or a jellyfish. What record does *L. longissimus* hold?

3. This particular species of trees is known for their enormous height. As of 2019, the tallest specimen is the one called Hyperion in an undisclosed location in California that touches the sky at an incredible 379.7 feet (approx. 115.7 m). These species of trees are known as Sequoioideae but have a common name, thanks to Spanish explorers who saw this tree for the first time and gave it its name because of the bright colour of the heartwood. By what name are these giants known?

4. In 1998, a specimen appropriately called Tyson from this extremely powerful species punched a hole in the quarter-inch-thick glass container it was held in. These animals have a formidable weapon in the form of claws that they usually keep folded away. When required, they unfurl it at an incredible speed of 80 km/hr, which is one of the fastest limb movements in the animal kingdom. Humans pale in comparison with the fastest boxer's hand moving at a relatively sedate 52 km/hr. Further, the animal does this underwater, which is far denser than air. By lashing out and retrieving the claw in under three thousandths of a second, it stuns the prey and would easily stun Mike Tyson, after whom that specimen has been named. What are these amazing animals that have the fastest claws in the world?

5. The biggest flying animal on earth is also one that is able to cover extraordinary distances in one flight. These birds have an astonishing wingspan of 8 feet to 11 feet in length, with one bird reported to have a wingspan of 17 feet 5 inches. These birds, true to their name, travel a lot, with some individuals known to have circumnavigated the Southern Ocean three times, covering more than 120,000 km in one year. They have been known to cover more than 5,500 km on a single trip, which is possible thanks to a process known as 'dynamic soaring'. Though their name might indicate that they do not know where they are flying to, the truth is that they have a disciplined flight path. What is the name of this incredibly well-travelled animal?

6. Jonathan was first brought to the island of Seychelles in 1882 and at that time, he was around fifty years old. There is a photograph of him from 1886, ambling around the official residence of the governor of St. Helena. As of 2019, he is still under the care of the government of St. Helena. Tu'i Malila was gifted by Captain James Cook to the royal family of Tonga when he arrived there in 1777. She was in the care of the Tongan royal family till 1965, when she passed away due to natural causes. Adwaita is supposed to have lived with Robert Clive in 1770s and was transferred to the Alipore zoo in Kolkata in 1875. He died of liver

failure in 2006. To which amazingly long-lived animal species do Jonathan, Tu'i Malila and Adwaita belong to?

7. *Archilochus colubris* is a common type of a certain bird species found in North America. Although averaging only about 3 inches in size, it holds the record for the fastest-ever wing-beat at an astonishing 200 beats per second. The species, by itself, is known by a particular name because all of them have an average wing-beat of 90 beats per second, which produces a particular sound. Of these, the *A.colubris* is an outstanding specimen. What species does it belong to?

8. The longest snake in the world is an eighteen-year-old reticulated python, which is owned by Full Moon Productions Inc in Kansas, USA. It measures an astonishing 7.67 metres (approx. 25 feet 2 inches) long. People who see it for the first time have been known to just stop in their tracks and freeze at the sight. This, coupled with the fact that it is a snake, is probably the reason for its name that has been given. What is the snake's name that is taken from Greek mythology?

9. The largest living cat in the world as of 2019 is Hercules, who is 3.33 metres (10.9 feet) long and weighs 418 kg. He eats 13.6 kg of meat per day to sustain himself and lives in South Carolina, USA. Hercules is quite a rare specimen that couldn't have existed in the wild, as his father and mother belong to different species, which

do not live together in the wild. If Hercules is a type of animal known as a Liger, what animals were his father and mother?

10. When measuring sound, it is done by decibels (dB), which increase logarithmically. When a Boeing 737 takes off, it produces 97 dB, which is four times as loud as a car going at 80 km/hr. Jill Drake, a classroom assistant from the UK, holds the Guinness World Record for the loudest scream at an ear-splitting 129 dB, enough to puncture all her students' ears if heard for more than 30 seconds. But the loudest known vocal sound made by an animal is an astonishing 188 dB. This ensures it can be heard from more than 800 kilometres away but not by humans, as it is at a guttural 20Hz, which is below the level of human hearing. Which animal that you would expect to be in this list in another capacity is able to produce such a loud sound?

11. The Taurus scarab is a species of a particular beetle, which measures just about 6 to 1 millimetres in length. They come from a particular family that gets its name because of the fact that they rely on the feces of other animals for their diet. This beetle is on this list because in a study done in 2010 by researchers from the University of London, it was shown to be the strongest animal in the world. Relative to its size, it could pull 1,141 times its own body weight. That is the equivalent

of a 70-kg human being able to lift 80 tons, which is about the weight of six buses. What lowly sounding family does this extraordinarily strong beetle come from?

12. *Chironex fleckeri* is a type of jellyfish found in the southern hemisphere, which has been described as the most venomous animal in the world. It is a translucent box about the size of a basketball, with fifteen 10-feet-long tentacles which, on contact, release microscopic darts that deliver an extremely powerful venom. Being stung commonly results in excruciating pain, and if the sting area is significant, an untreated victim may die in two to five minutes. The sting is so painful that it is usually followed by a cardiac arrest. Due to the nature of this jellyfish, it has a common name that refers to where it is found and an insect that also has painful stings. What is the common name of *C. fleckeri*?

13. The South American basilisk lizard can run at a speed of 1.5 m/s (5 ft/s), which is quite fast for a reptile, but what sets it apart is the where it is able to achieve this feat. This remarkable ability has earned it the moniker of 'Jesus Christ Lizard', which refers to a particular miraculous event that Christ had performed when a ship full of disciples was caught in a storm in the Sea of Galilee. What is the unique ability of the basilisk lizard?

14. The Colossal squid is the largest known invertebrate ever known in history. From the few specimens caught,

it has been known to be about 45 feet in length and weigh around 750 kilograms. The extraordinary size is attributed to a phenomenon known as 'abyssal gigantism,' where invertebrates tend to be much larger due to the colder temperature, food scarcity and extreme pressure at the depths where they usually live. Due to this, a certain body part has evolved in the colossal squid to massive dimensions. The body part is estimated to be at least 30 to 40 centimetres (12 in to 16 in) in diameter. Compared to that, the average human version is a microscopic 24 millimetres in diameter. What body part is this that dwarfs ours in the Colossal Squid?

15. Mammals are some of the most voracious eaters in the animal kingdom, and in terms of food amount to body size, these tiny mole-like animals are the biggest eaters among mammals. Every day, they have to eat up to three times their own weight in order to survive, as compared to elephants, for example, which eat just about 1/20th of their weight in food. Though they look like long-nosed mice or rats, they are more closely related to hedgehogs. What animal is this, which is the only animal to be mentioned in the title of a Shakespearean play?

ANSWERS

1. Peregrine Falcon
2. Longest animal in the world
3. Redwood trees
4. Mantis Shrimp
5. Wandering Albatross
6. Tortoises
7. Hummingbird
8. Medusa
9. Lion and tigress
10. Blue Whale
11. Dung Beetle
12. Sea Wasp
13. Run/walk on water
14. Eyes
15. Shrew

11. PHRASES AND IDIOMS

1. This particular phrase was used to describe the legendary boxer Muhammad Ali and is thought to have been coined by his trainer, Drew Brown. It beautifully describes Ali's swift and light footwork and lethal jabs. What is the phrase that references not one but two animals starting with the same letter?

2. This particular phrase refers to an overreaction to a trivial matter. It refers to two natural formations: one a geological formation and another a formation made by a certain burrowing animal. What is this seven-word phrase?

3. This phrase refers to one of the most basic natural phenomena in the world—one that all our ancestors must have noticed! It is likely to have been associated with safety, warmth and light, hence its present-day association in English with someone or something who 'brings joy or hope'. What three-word phrase is this that makes you think of the sun?

4. This phrase, used to refer to someone who prefers to avoid facing unpleasant facts, comes from an early legend that a certain animal would carry out a certain action in the belief that this would hide it from the people around. Of course, the animals don't really do this! The legend may have arisen due to the fact that their eggs are laid under the ground and the parents often check on them. What is this phrase and the animal?

5. This collective noun is used to refer to a group of flamingoes. It starts with the same letter and may refer to the sheer magnificence of these creatures strutting around together. What is this eleven-letter word?

6. This animal is used across the world and across cultures in agriculture and to draw heavy objects. This may explain why, if you want to talk about someone's strength, you compare them to this animal. What is the phrase that you would use?

7. This phrase is used to describe a state of nervousness, where it may indeed feel like one's interior is full of a fluttering! What is the phrase that sounds a lot more poetic than it may feel?

8. This particular phrase is still quite popular when used to describe someone who has poor eyesight (or to imply that someone has bad eyesight!). However, the irony is that the animal used in the comparison actually has very good eyesight! What is this phrase?

The Amazing Nature Quiz • 73

9. This proverb plays on the fact that these animals are quite hard to catch. Thus, if you have managed to catch a specimen, hang on to it rather than letting it go in order to have two hands free for two more specimens somewhere else! What is this proverb?

10. This popular question is used to indicate a situation where it is hard to figure out the order in which things happened, because everything seems related! It refers to the cyclical argument that a certain object could not have appeared without another object appearing before it, but the latter object needed the former to come into the world itself, and so on! What is this confusing question?

11. In the wild, these animals have been known to map out vast areas and remember specific locations such as watering holes from hundreds of kilometres away. In a study done in 2007, it was shown that each of these animals could recognize the urine of thirty of their companions. In 1999, two specimens were brought together, and they became very animated and started socializing. It was discovered later that they remembered each other from a short stint of a few months they had both spent together in a circus. These are examples which back up what phrase about a species of animal?

12. It has often been stated that without a sense of smell, apples, onions and potatoes taste the same (you can

try this!). However, apples are definitely distinct from another fruit. So different, in fact, that this phrase is often used when someone tries to equate two things that are utterly unrelated! What is this phrase?

13. This phrase is used to determine how much of a certain element is produced by any particular action. This specific element has long been associated with global warming and governments all over the world *must* start taking it more seriously now and reducing their _____ _____ in order to help people live more eco-friendly lives, to ensure the planet actually survives! What is this two-word phrase?

14. All mammals are subject to the Henneman's size principle, which essentially states that the smallest muscles are the ones that are activated first. This minimizes the fatigue an animal experiences and permits fine control of force. One mammal, however, does not follow this principle and is able to access the larger muscles first and, thereby, have really fast reactions. What phrase comes about because of this that one would usually use to describe acrobats or sport people?

15. To round off this set of nature-inspired idioms, what would you be doing if you went off to answer a 'call of nature'?

ANSWERS

1. Floats like a butterfly, stings like a bee
2. Making a mountain out of a molehill
3. Ray of light
4. Burying your head in the sand, ostrich
5. A 'flamboyance' of flamingoes
6. Strong as an ox
7. Butterflies in your stomach
8. Blind as a bat
9. A bird in hand is worth two in the bush
10. What came first? The chicken or the egg?
11. Elephants never forget
12. Comparing apples and oranges
13. Carbon footprint
14. Cat-like reflexes
15. Using the restroom!

12. WACKY WILDLIFE

1. The axolotl is a type of Mexican salamander that has a very unusual development method. Unlike other amphibians, they do not undergo metamorphosis and develop lungs to survive on land. Axolotls reach adulthood without growing up; they retain their gills and remain aquatic. They also have fantastic regeneration ability, being able to rebuild jaws, spines and even brains without any scarring. This ability to 'not grow up' and have efficient regeneration has led to the axolotl being compared to a fictional character from a popular children's book. Who is this child who never grew up, who the axolotl gets compared to?

2. The wombat is a small marsupial found in Australia, where they dig extensive burrow systems. Their pouches face backward to ensure that when digging, they don't get soil inside the pouch. The most interesting thing about them is the way they mark their territory. They usually stay inside the burrow, but when they do go out to forage for food, they leave distinctively-shaped

poop outside to let other wombats know about their burrow. Since most of the area is hilly, the distinctive shape, which looks very unnatural, ensures that it does not roll off. In what peculiar shape do wombats poop?

3. This particular fish has a very interesting life-cycle. All fishes of this species are born with both male and female parts (scientifically hermaphrodites). In the colony, the largest fish is the female and the second largest is the male, while all the others are both. If the female dies, the male turns into a female and one of the smaller ones becomes a male. Scientists have put this unique system down to the fact that these animals all live in a very small space around sea anemones, and if the female were lost it would be near impossible for the colony to find another female in the vicinity. With this unique ability to change their sex, the colony ensures the safety of the community. Which fish is this, whose actual life story is very different from the way a very popular children's movie had shown them?

4. These animals are known for their strange ways of standing and the way they eat, which is to sift water upside down. The most striking part of their look is the characteristic colour of their plumage—so much so that certain shades of this colour are named in this animal's honour. Interestingly, the animals are naturally white, and they get their characteristic colour only because of their diet. The colour comes from a natural

dye called canthaxanthin, which is found in the brine shrimp and blue-green algae that are the main food sources for these animals. To ensure that they retain the colour, zoos usually add artificial canthaxanthin, or else they would become white. Which animal is this that is usually seen in huge numbers in salty lakes?

5. *Litoria 'X'* is a frog that was discovered by accident in 2008 by a herpetologist in the Foja Mountains in Indonesia. It has the ability to enlarge and inflate its nose when the male frog is calling out, which has led to it being called by a particular name that references a character from a popular fairy tale, who had similar issues but under different circumstances. In 2019, it was finally given the same name as its species name as well. What is its name?

6. These animals are seen as cute and adorable the world over and are usually a big attraction in zoos. They are extremely clever and are known to use rocks as tools to get to their favourite foods. One of the most endearing features is how they sleep. Since they are usually afloat, they hold hands with each other when asleep to ensure they don't drift apart in the current. This has spawned many cute memes and images, which are easy to find on the internet. What very fascinating species of animals are these?

7. The characteristic look of this animal helps break up the outline of its body, making it hard to see when

it's stalking its prey. It also looks like shadows in the moonlight, hence disguising the presence of the animal. Interestingly, not only the fur but the skin underneath as well has the same characteristic and the pattern is unique to each individual. What animals are these, whose striking features usually bring fear to any animal in their path?

8. While handling these animals at a wildlife park in Adelaide, an anthropologist realized that their fingers carried ridged patterns of loops, whorls and arches unique to each individual just like those on a human hand. The only difference is the layout, as the hands of this animal are adapted for climbing and thus have three digits facing forward and two facing sideward. What animals are these that live on a steady diet of Eucalyptus leaves?

9. This animal holds many records, but the most amazing one is that it has the world's slowest digestion. These animals evolved to expend very little energy, because their diet does not provide them a lot of nutrition. This is because the leaves they usually eat are full of toxins, which these animals have evolved to digest. They have multi-chambered stomachs with a variety of bacteria that break down the leaves, but it takes a long time. It takes almost two weeks to digest one meal, which makes it the slowest digestion of any mammal. Which animal is this that takes things very slowly?

10. This is a genus of flying lizards, which technically glide by jumping off trees, making them technically Leaping Lizards. Carl Linnaeus derived the name of this genus from the Latin term for mythological dragons. Some of the younger readers of this book may recognize the genus name from another fictional character, who, in his case, flew with assistance from a household cleaning device. What diabolical sounding genus is this?

11. The coastal region of Kutch in Gujarat is a large desert and has two breeds of camel. One is the popular Kutchi breed and the other is the Kharai breed, which is only found in this region. Recognized as a separate breed by the National Bureau of Animal Genetic Resources, the Kharai camel is probably the only domesticated breed of camel that lives in dual ecosystems. It has a unique ability to head out in to the gulf and feed on saline plants and mangroves, sometimes travelling more than 3 kilometres. This characteristic has given it the moniker of '_____ camel', which brings a completely new meaning to the phrase 'Ship of the desert'. What is the moniker?

12. Although for many years cartoons, children's books and even movies have been showing this event, the truth is that this animal is incapable of jumping. This makes it the only land animal with legs that is incapable of getting all its legs off the floor at the same time. One

reason is because of the weight of the animal, but the underlying reason is that unlike in other mammals, the bones in this animal are all pointed downwards, which means that they do not have the 'spring' required to push off the ground. Which animal is this that prefers to have its feet firmly on solid ground?

13. The unique characteristic of these animals is thanks to the presence of E-2-butenee-1-thiol, 3-methyl-1-butanethiol and 2-quinoline wmethanethiol, which are low-molecular weight thiol compounds. Combined with a few more acetate thioesters, these can be detected by a human nose at miniscule concentrations of ten parts per billion. Which animal is this, that has a characteristic colour pattern as well due to this marvelous nature but has been vilified in many cartoons and movies?

14. This animal's eyes are about the size of billiard balls, giving them excellent vision, which is required to keep an eye out for predators in the vast plains they inhabit. Unfortunately, these eyes take up so much space in the head that the brain size is compromised and it is actually smaller than the eyeballs. This might explain why it's not very smart and tends to run around in circles when running away from a predator. Which animal is this that is known for having 'big' records in other departments but unfortunately not in brain size?

15. In 2013, a song called 'What Does the Fox Say?' became a hit, and although it mentions a lot of animal sounds, it is scientifically untrue, as foxes make a variety of sounds such as barking, yelping and snarling. There is one animal, though, which is not mentioned in the song and actually does not make any audible noise. Previously, it was believed that maybe the animals made very low frequency sounds (like elephants), so it couldn't be heard by humans. Another theory was that though they have a larynx, they weren't able to produce sufficient airflow through their 4 metre long trachea to actually vocalize. Only recently have researchers discovered that these animals, in fact, keep doing something that content humans do when they are bored—they keep humming. Which animals are these that deserved to be the focus of that song (which is very hummable to be honest)?

ANSWERS

1. Peter Pan
2. Cubes
3. Clownfish
4. Flamingos
5. Pinocchio frog
6. Sea otters
7. Tiger

8. Koala bears
9. Sloth
10. Draco
11. Swimming camels
12. Elephants
13. Skunk
14. Ostrich
15. Giraffe

ACKNOWLEDGEMENTS

I would like to thank my grandmother, Mrs Charlotte Winifred, for introducing me to the fascinating world of nature. As I used to crawl around on all fours, following random ants around the house, she taught me to study them and figure out what they were doing, but not disturb them. I was lucky to grow up in a house that had an abundance of plants and animals, which were identified and taught to me diligently by her.

My love for nature increased exponentially as I started reading. Gerald Durrell and James Herriot were two authors who forever shaped my mind to not just think about animals but also to care for them and their well-being. It would be criminal of me to leave David Attenborough out, as even now I cannot imagine a natural scene without his characteristic voice bringing to words the beauty that is in front of me.

I would like to thank the staff of the Zoology department, The American College, Madurai, for putting up with my outrageous behaviour for three years and still managing to teach me amazing things about the natural world.

Last but not least I'd like to thank Spook Bono Barett Woodhead 'd' P Ashley. He was my best friend, my partner-in-crime and the brother who would always watch out for me. He taught me that morality, goodness, selflessness and empathy were not unique to humans. Thank you Spook for fourteen years of companionship that I shall remember forever. You were a good boy.

Berty

I have been lucky enough to grow up in two very green cities, both of which had their share of animal and bird-life thriving within the city! One of my earliest memories is of waiting for a specific bird to come perch on a gladiolus flower outside our window—every time the flowers came out, along came this bird! Moving to Chennai introduced me to different kinds of trees and birds. My school, Kalakshetra, was a splendid place for children to learn about the natural world, and life in a coastal city fills one with wonder for water and sky and all the creatures that thrive in the depths of the oceans! I would like to thank my parents and grandparents for developing in me not only appreciation, but also respect for the world around me. Finally, I would like to especially thank my mother for sharing her enthusiasm for nature and nature writing, and both my grandmothers, whose green thumbs and passion for things that grow shaped my own love for plants and trees.

Akhila